Faith Rebuilt

A 30-Day Devotional Journey to Strengthen Your Faith

April McDuffie

**And they overcame him by the blood of the Lamb, and by the word of their testimony.
Revelation 12:11**

xulon
PRESS

www.xulonpress.com

In Memory of Darlene Branam

"Do not look at this as defeat but
unto His glory."

Acknowledgements

Thank you to my husband, Wayne, and daughter, Cali, for always being right there beside me. These two are the loves of my life. I am so glad what God is doing in our little family!

To my parents, Danny and Pam Gay, and parents-in-law, Dobie and Teressa McDuffie: Thank you for always being there for us—loving us and praying for us. Thank you for serving as Godly examples.

Throughout this journey, there were many people who encouraged me and upheld me in prayer: the FAB 5, our Pastor

Dewain Joiner, Fitzgerald Church of God, all of our C³ Children's department, and many other friends.

Thank you to Deborah Smith for being my "editor," and Alice B. Hobson for being Alice B.!

Thank you to my writing mentor Joyce Ashley. She got what my heart was trying to say! God has ordained our friendship for such a time as this.

Most of all, Thank You to my Abba Father. Thank You for Your mercies that are new each day. I pray that I will always be obedient to Your voice.

Foreword

"JOY IN THE LORD!" Those are the words I have often used to describe my friend, April McDuffie. She exemplifies JOY in the Lord! With a constant, radiant smile on her face, April approaches each day with a strong faith in God and a willingness to serve Him at every opportunity.

When she asked me to read her "devotional journey," I was delighted! She had never shared with me that she was a writer, too! It came as a complete surprise (a JOYful one) that God had given her the vision for this book. Even more shocking was the revelation of April's "secret." She was struggling with pain and sometimes doubted that God would do anything about it! As I witnessed the complete transparency with which she allowed her heart to be spilled out onto the pages of this book, a new love and admiration for my friend began to well up in my own heart. How could she be such a joyful, Godly example when she was privately dealing with such levels of pain and such circumstances that caused heartache? I began to see the pieces of the puzzle fit together as I read of her continual choice to believe...in a faithful God!

In this beautifully written story of faith, you will find an up-close and personal look into the heart of a woman who is sold out to Christ. What a refreshing, encouraging message she offers. Life is *not* always easy, but we have the promise of The One Who tells us He will "never leave us or forsake us" (Deuteronomy 31:6). Each of us finds ourselves in need of a "faith booster" from time to time. No matter how long we have been Christians, we need the encouragement of those who have "been there, done that" and are willing to share their stories about what God has taught them along their journey. This book is exactly that: a brief but powerful episode in the true struggle of April McDuffie's life. Instead of giving up on her faith when it might have been easier to do so, she stood firm and did not allow the enemy to steal her joy or defeat her faith! She has chosen to learn the lessons God wanted to teach her through her trials and difficulties. Now, she has been obedient in putting them into book form so that we, too, may be reminded of the truth of scripture and the faithfulness of God.

For the next 30 days, allow the Lord to touch your heart by using this book of devotionals that you now hold in your hand. May it be a friendly companion and a delicious "appetizer" to cause you to hunger for the Truth that can be found in His Word. I am convinced that April would want me to remind you that NO BOOK is a replacement for THE BOOK—His book, The Holy Bible. However, God has blessed April with a wisdom and depth of understanding that she has skillfully penned for us all to read and, hopefully, receive our own personal revelations.

Now, turn the page and begin the journey of rebuilding your faith!

Joyce Ashley, founder of JoyJoy Ministries

Author of *JOY JUICE: Delightful Flavors of JOY in the Lord* and *ABUNDANT JOY JUICE, Squeezed from God's Word*

Voice of JOY JUICE Radio Outreach, and partner of Team RADIATE

Table of Contents

Introduction

November 12, 2011

*H*ebrews 11:1 states, "Now faith is the substance of things hoped for, the evidence of things not seen." (KJV) As a minister's wife, I have often quoted that very scripture to friends, family, church members, coworkers, and even strangers. I have prayed with and for others that were struggling through some of life's worst moments—ones that needed physical, financial, or emotional healing. Praying for ones that were facing death's door, I claimed their healing without any hesitation and with all expectation that they would be healed. Even though our mortal minds cannot comprehend how massive our God is, I know that He is big enough to move in miraculous ways with His miraculous power. However, I have come to the realization that I have unshaken faith for others but am unable to have this same faith myself.

In September 2009, I had tests for some gastrointestinal problems I had off and on for two years. The next week, I experienced a week of storms that seemed to rage endlessly. My husband is a children's pastor, and one of our young teens at church was found to be in a situation that would shake and destroy anyone's life and family that Monday morning. On Monday afternoon, I got called to my mother's house to find that she had cancer. I felt numbness sinking into my mind, heart, and soul. That evening at home, one of my best friends stopped by to tell me she had filed for divorce from her husband of 23 years. I sincerely tried but my spirit was struggling to advise, to love, to guide, to listen. Two hours passed, and my unmarried sister, along with a friend, came by the house to confide that she was expecting a baby. At that time, my spirit was deadened. None of this was happening to me personally. However the weights upon my shoulders were suffocating me. I told my husband there were no more tears, no more emotions, no more thoughts. As a mother, wife, and a dean of a college, my personality was to always solve the problem— figure out the solution and implement it, quickly and effectively. Only now, I merely wanted my husband to hold me until I went to sleep.

The next day, all the events from the day before were still there. It was not a dream, and it was time to face the day. My main focus would be on my mother overcoming her cancer. Later that afternoon, I left work early to go to the doctor to get the results from my personal tests. When I got there, I was informed my doctor had left sick for the day and I needed to reschedule for the next week. I asked if another doctor in the group could see me, and the receptionist stated there were no available appointments. It took everything inside me not to just sit down and scream in the middle of the waiting room until someone saw me that day. I knew if I started crying, I would not stop. I asked to see the office manager, a friend and church member, and she got a nurse to see me who in return stopped a doctor in the hall. He confirmed that I needed to see a surgeon to have my gallbladder removed. The very next day, I visited a surgeon who scheduled me for preop on Friday and surgery the following Monday. I have known many people that have had this surgery with quick recovery and just a few days missed from work. This would be a perfect plan as I would have the surgery and recover before my mother faced her surgery and, in addition, my college was on fall break.

I proceeded with my surgery on Monday, and everything was fine. My husband stayed home with me that day, and then I was at the house the rest of the week by myself. The recovery was harder than I expected, but I knew I was going to be ready to go back to work the next week. The next Monday I drove to one of our campuses out of town for a meeting and began feeling nauseated and having continuous sharp pains internally. One of my coworkers drove me home, and the doctor's office consulted me on what to do—basically take pain and nausea medicine. The only time the pain would go away was during sleep. During the next few days, this same pain came and went without reasoning, mostly during the night and lasting 30 minutes or so at a time. Nothing appeared to touch this excruciating pain—medicine, heating pad, prayers, or crying out to God claiming and begging for healing.

The week after my surgery, my mother had her surgery. The doctor was able to remove all of her cancer. Beginning that afternoon and over the next few weeks, I would visit the surgeon to try to identify my pain. Since that first visit, I have had over 20 visits to 10 different doctors including out of state, countless tests, endless medicines to try, visits to the ER, and one ICU overnight stay. After one procedure, what I have begun to refer to as "spasms" stopped but only to return six days later.

Since September 2009, my mother has battled two rounds of cancer but has been cancer free since August 2010. My sister is married and has a beautiful little boy that has captured my heart. My friend has been Biblically released from a horrible marriage and has a new freedom in life. I have not remained in contact with the young teen or her family but pray for her from time-to-time. Funny how we get knocked off our feet so easily when so much is thrown at us at one time. If we could only remember that God is control of each situation, and when we look back, everything will be taken care of in *His* time and *His* way.

Now, November 2011, 26 months after having my gallbladder removed, my spasms occur anywhere from 1 to 5 times daily. No doctor has been able to identify the source of the spasms or how to prevent or stop them from happening. One doctor did pre-scribe nitroglycerin to take on the onset of the spasm, which cuts the spasms to 5-10 minutes—which is wonderful compared to 30 minutes. The funniest part is that a 37-year old woman takes up to 50 nitro-glycerins a month! When anyone would ask how I was, I would tell them that I was fine. A few friends and family, close coworkers, and my pastor are the only ones that even know about the spasms. Only my husband knows the extent to which the spasms have altered my life, the severe pain during the middle of the night, the struggle of the end-less doctors' appointments to stop the pain, and the tears I have shed. I have requested prayer a couple of times and been prayed over at the altar of my church, but this body is still not healed.

Through these last two years, I have prayed for healing, but I know I felt in my heart that the spasms would stop once the doctors did this next procedure, this next medicine, this new specialist. I would claim healing in words, but I know I did not believe in my heart for an immediate healing from God. I have stated that I was called to be April McDuffie, not the apostle Paul. Paul was called to accept *his* thorn in *his* flesh. I do not have that same calling and do not have to accept this. I have said all of the right words and prayed all of the right prayers. However, my faith is waivered.

Over the last week, I have felt in my spirit that I need to enter a 30-day faith promise. I feel I am to write a faith journal over the next 30 days of how God has healed me— claiming as if I am already healed. The New Living Translation translates Hebrews 11:1

as, "Faith is the confidence that what we hope for will actually happen; it gives us assurance about things we cannot see." Through this journey, through this act of obedience, my hope is to develop that very confidence in my faith that I will be healed. The doctor's next plan is to send me to a university in South Carolina for further testing. My next plan is to discard my nitroglycerin, sleep through an entire night, and be a witness of God's miraculous power to still perform miracles today.

The following pages are daily devotionals I wrote during my 30-day journey. God has led me to share these devotions to guide others through any faith crisis encountered. Each devotion has an area for you to journalize your reflections as well. My prayer is that you will strengthen your faith in the One that has the answers to all of your needs. May you continuously feel His power and His strength as you begin *your* journey. At the end of these 30 days, may your faith be rebuilt.

Join online at:

www.facebook.com/FaithRebuilt

Day 1

Through him you believe in God, who raised him from the dead and glorified him, and so your faith and hope are in God.

1 Peter 1:21 (NIV)

God was in existence before anything. He spoke and created the world and everything in it. He sent His son to this earth to die for us. Jesus arose from the grave after three days. If we ask Him to forgive us of our sin and accept Him as our Savior, we are born again and become a

Christian. As a Christian, when we die, we go to live with Him for eternity in Heaven.

These are the fundamental truths of our Christian beliefs, even though none of us have seen anything of this with our own eyes. Yet, we fully believe in every aspect of our Christian faith. Hebrews 11:1 (KJV) states, "Now faith is the substance of things hoped for, the evidence of things not seen." Our belief in these fundamental truths is the ultimate faith in action.

Why is it that we have seen evidence of God's power with our own eyes and still do not have the faith we need? We have seen ones who have life-threatening illnesses miraculously recover, and the doctors have no explanation. Some have had tests that show a medical problem, yet when further testing was conducted, the problem was already gone. We know and trust that God moved in such situations. We have praised

Him and worshipped Him for answering prayers, and never doubt that it was He.

Why then, do we have little faith for God to supply what we need in our personal life? Through Him we believe that He is our God, and we must rest in the fact that our faith lies totally in Him. Just as you trust Him for who He is, trust Him for the answers you need.

My reflections of my personal journey

_____

_____

_____

_____

_____

_____

_____

Day 2

But may the God of all grace, who called us to His eternal glory by Christ Jesus, after you have suffered a while, perfect, establish, strengthen, and settle you.
1 Peter 5:10

God's Word does not say that we would never encounter struggles, pain, hardship, or trials. In fact, throughout the Bible, we are given countless stories to read and learn about God's deliverance, protection, and guidance. 1 Peter 5:10

reminds us that even while we may suffer, through His grace, God will strengthen and sustain us. Think about the Israelites. After 40 years of wondering in the wilderness, the promise land was theirs for the taking. When Job lost everything he had, God replenished everything double-fold due to Job's faithfulness.

Jesus said that in this life, we will have tribulations. It is our human nature to question why and how much longer must we endure this trial. In our small town, we have an annual Relay for Life. Each year, I am amazed at the list of names announced for memorials and honorariums. I know so many of those names of the people that have battled cancer. I see the survivors during the survivor walk and the families during the memorial lap. These families have suffered greatly.

I think about how Jesus suffered the day He died on the cross—for me and you. Even He asked, "My God, My God, why have you forsaken me?" (Matthew 27:46). We must realize that God has a purpose for everything in our lives. Through our time of suffering, we learn patience, humbleness, faith, and reliance on our Father. We often learn more of God's plan for our life as we go through this time. Just as Jesus' suffering was not in vain, neither will ours be.

My reflections of my personal journey

_____

_____

_____

_____

_____

_____

Day 3

But he was wounded for our transgressions, he was bruised for our iniquities: the chastisement of our peace was upon him; and with his stripes we are healed.
Isaiah 53:5

Music has always been a part of my life—from traveling in a singing group at age 3, joining the church choir at age 12, active in my high school music program, leading the choir as an adult, and now working with the children in the children's department. It is a joke at my house to give me a word, and I will either think of an existing song to sing or make one completely up using that word. I always have a song in my heart!

This verse was the basis of a chorus that my childhood church sang regularly:

He was wounded for our transgressions.
He was bruised for our iniquities.
Surely He bore our sorrows.
And by His stripes we are healed.

Whenever I experienced spasms in my body, I would sing this song. Sometimes I would hum it; sometimes I would cry it out in the shower in desperate plea.

Over 2000 years ago, Jesus left His glorious home and walked among us—to live as us, to talk with us, to teach us. Knowing He would die a horrible, humiliating death,

He did so for the very reasons listed in this verse. While He was on that cross, His blood flowed. The blood was shed for our remissions of our sin and for our healing— for mine and for yours. Have you believed in the power of His blood for your healing? If not, do so today. It was the power behind my healing!

My reflections of my personal journey

_____

_____

_____

_____

_____

_____

_____

_____

_____

Day 4

Aware of their discussion, Jesus asked them: "Why are you talking about having no bread? Do you still not see or understand? Are your hearts hardened? Do you have eyes but fail to see, and ears but fail to hear? And don't you remember?... He said to them, "Do you still not understand?"
Mark 8:17-18, 21 (NIV)

*H*ow amazing it must have been to walk with the Master! To see Him teaching! To witness Him performing miracles! Can you imagine being one of Jesus' chosen 12? One would think since the disciples had actually seen with their own eyes and heard with their own ears, they would never face any doubt, fear, or worry. However, time and time again, we see where the disciples lost their faith which often prevented clarity and understanding of Jesus' teaching.

How often has Jesus reminded you of all of the miracles He has performed in your life or when He has moved in situations when you asked? Why, then, do we not trust Him to have complete control of our lives?

Throughout our lives, we will have times where we do not understand why things are happening—why we lost our job, why we are not healed, why we lost someone we loved so early...why, why, why. We must remember how God has moved and answered prayers throughout our lives. Through this, we have confidence in God that, even though we may not understand, we know that God has a plan. All through the ages, He has taken care of His people, honoring them that worship Him. We must remember—He will do it again!

My reflections of my personal journey

_____

_____

_____

_____

_____

_____

_____

_____

Day 5

Give thanks to the LORD, for he is good! His faithful love endures forever.
Psalms 107:1 (NLT)

"Thank you, Lord! Thank you, Lord!" I have been a member of my church for over 18 years. Throughout this time, there have been two women that I knew could pray and touch Heaven's throne room for me. One just recovered from surgery to remove colon cancer. The other just passed away this week. A close group of us were reminiscing this week about her and were laughing about how we used to pick on her for repeating in her prayers, "Father God, Father God." However, when I read this verse tonight, I could hear her say, "Thank you, Lord! Thank you, Lord!" When she prayed with someone at the altar, toward the end of her prayer, she would claim the answer to that prayer and begin to thank God as if it had already come to pass. What faith she had!

What if we all did that? What if we thanked God as if it has come to pass? I have heard and even said it myself, "Thank you, God, for what you are going   to do." What if we thank Him as if it has already happened? "Thank you, God, for what you HAVE done in this situation. Thank you, God, for healing my body. Thank you, God, for saving my lost loved one." My faith journal started five days ago, and I thank

God for healing me of the spasms. I thank Him that my body is healed completely and that I do not have to take nitroglycerin anymore. I thank Him that I can be a witness to His healing power!

Where do you need God to move in your life? What struggle are you going through or what answer do you need? Go ahead and thank Him! You see, He is going to move; He is going to answer. He said so in His Word. Don't worry—just thank Him!

My reflections of my personal journey

_____

_____

_____

_____

_____

Day 6

Jesus answered, "It is written: 'Man does not live on bread alone, but on every word that comes from the mouth of God.'"
Matthew 4:4 (NIV)

No matter what problem you are facing, you can find your answer in God's word. When Jesus was in the wilderness, He fasted and prayed for 40 days and nights. During this time, the devil tempted over and over. One of the temptations was to turn the stone into bread; he thought that

Jesus' physical body was hungry. What the devil did not know is that His spiritual body would never hunger as He was the Bread of Life.

During a two-year period when my body was struggling, I had pain/spasms that seemed to come whenever I was hungry—actually, if my stomach was just empty. One month, our Pastor called us to a 21-day fast. I could not fast due to the pain it would cause. I fasted anything to drink but water. However, I wanted to give my all during that time. Through faith, I was able to replace this time of pain and "hunger" through the Word of God. By feasting on His word, my faith increased and complete healing came to my body.

What do you hunger for? Is it a healing you need? Is it an answer that you are awaiting? Are you looking for a closer walk in your relationship with God? Are you struggling to find the path He has chosen for you? His promises just for you are already written in His Word. Open it, read it, and let Him speak to you today!

My reflections of my personal journey

_____

_____

_____

_____

_____

_____

_____

_____

_____

_____

_____

_____

_____

Day 7

And behold, the veil of the temple was torn in two from top to bottom; and the earth shook and the rocks were split.
Matthew 27:51 (NASB)

*O*f everything recorded in God's word, this is perhaps the most poignant part to me. When Jesus was on the cross, our Savior sacrificed His life in the most horrific crucifixion. The moment He gave up His spirit and died, there was a large earthquake, and people, including one of the soldiers, realized He must have been the Son of God. At the very moment He died, the veil of the temple was torn and ripped from top to bottom. The veil of the temple had separated the Holy of Holies, where God's presence dwelt, from the rest of the temple where men were allowed. Now that the veil is torn, we all may enter into the Holy of Holies. We can boldly approach the throne of God, make our petitions known, and dwell in His presence.

As we enter into His presence, we make our petitions known directly to Him—our hearts desires, our needs. As we dwell in His presence, our faith rises. Our fears are released and worries diminished. We are filled with His goodness, mercy, spirit, faith, and love. Enter into the Holy of Holies, dwell in His presence, and let your faith arise.

My reflections of my personal journey

Day 8

And he answered and said unto them, I tell you that, if these should hold their peace, the stones would immediately cry out.
Luke 19:40

When Jesus entered Jerusalem, the multitude began to praise Him. You see, they knew who was living among them. As they shouted in honor of their King, the Pharisees instructed Jesus to quiet the crowd. Jesus replied that the rocks would cry out if my people do not worship me.

Today, we still have Pharisees all around! Why do we allow such "Pharisees" to silence our praises? Is it because we have become too "modernized" in our walk with God and have determined that we are much more reserved or more sophisticated now? Or, do we have internal "Pharisees" such as doubt, worry, sin, and shame that prevent us from giving Him the praises He deserves.

I am a huge college football fan and an alumna of a large state university. I will "bark" my praises for my team all season—win or lose. I will shout, "Go Dawgs!" to a complete stranger if I see a person with a rival emblem on their attire. I am proud to be a part of the Bulldog nation. Do we praise our Christian team with as much passion as this? If we see a non-Christian on the "wrong" team, do we walk up to complete strangers to testify of the greatness of our God? Do we shout His praises in good times and in bad? We have the ultimate Coach, but are we a fan of His?

Starting today, go outside your private prayer talk with God; go outside your church service on Sunday and Wednesday. Shout His praises into every aspect in your life with everyone you meet. Praise God for your healing, for your life, for your family, for what you have and what you are going to have. Do not let a rock take your place!

My reflections of my personal journey

_____

_____

_____

_____

_____

_____

_____

Day 9

Search me, O God, and know my heart; test me and know my anxious thoughts. See if there is any offensive way in me, and lead me in the way everlasting.
Psalms 139:23-24 (NIV)

When Jesus healed the lame man, He instructed him to "go and sin no more." Throughout the Bible and all ages of time, God has performed miracles that our minds cannot comprehend. However, the greatest miracle of all is when someone receives salvation. When someone becomes a born-again Christian, it does not block sin from our life. We know that sometimes we may fail and sin. While we make mistakes and ask forgiveness of this sin, sin should not be habitual or predetermined. We must always refrain from evil and the appearances of evil.

Since I was saved at the age of five, my nightly prayers have included a statement for God to forgive me of any sins I have committed, including any that I was unaware of or forgotten that I had done, and to help me not make these mistakes again. One of the most Godly men that I have had the privilege of knowing was a retired minister in my church. I visited him just hours before he passed away. On his death bed in the hospital, he prayed, "Father please don't let there be anything separating me and you." WOW! This "saint" was making sure nothing was on his heart as he prepared to meet his Savior.

Psalms 139 is my favorite chapter in the Bible. Verses 23-24 remind us to refrain from any offensive way, any sin, and to follow in His everlasting path of righteousness. Does our faith stumble because we have any sin in our heart? I am not suggesting that people get sick because they sin. However, I wonder if we have sin in our heart, does that prevent our heart from fully trusting God for the answers we need? Do we block our own prayers of healing because our minds are ashamed of sin that we now have or even sin from our past that God has already forgiven? Ask God to search you, to forgive you, and forgive yourself. Free your mind and heart from the residue of sin and replace it with hope and faith!

My reflections of my personal journey

_____

_____

_____

_____

_____

_____

_____

_____

_____

_____

_____

_____

_____

_____

_____

_____

_____

_____

_____

Day 10

You are my hiding place; you will pro-tect me from trouble and surround me with songs of deliverance.
Psalms 32:7 (NIV)

$\mathcal{I}$ treated my daughter and two of her friends to a makeup consultation today. While they are all three beautiful and flawless, I know the time is approaching where they will want to wear a little makeup now and then. At one point, we discussed concealer—the makeup used to hide blemishes, uneven skin tone, and dark circles. With proper application, you would not know the flaws that lie beneath the makeup.

I thought about measures we go through to hide things in our own lives. I often see people smiling, even though I know their pain is great. In the current economy, people we see every day are struggling, yet would never admit it or ask for help. People in our world hide themselves with a mask they wear daily. Perhaps they are afraid for others to see their worry or their lack of faith. If only they knew that there is a God that is larger than any problem they will ever have. A God who knows the answer they need, can give the direction they need to take, and can strengthen their faith for them to make it through once again.

How quickly we forget that God is our refuge. We can peacefully rest under His wings. His is our Protector and our Victor.

When you are hurt, discouraged, alone, or afraid, do not try to conceal yourself or hide. Run to Him. Find your hiding place in Him. Shout His praises. He will fill you with songs of victory!

My reflections of my personal journey

_____

_____

_____

_____

_____

_____

_____

_____

_____

_____

_____

Day 11

The Lord is my shepherd; I have all that I need.
Psalms 23:1 (NLV)

*O*h, the blessings of God. Everywhere we look, we see Him. From the moment we wake up in the morning, we see Him all day long. We have breath to live! We serve a good God, a Father that cares for us, a Shepherd that provides for us. So often we compare what we have to what others have. That is where we are wrong. If we follow and serve God, we have *exactly* what He wants us to have. It is hard to comprehend, but He knows more about us than we do ourselves. How many times have we prayed for God to intervene in our lives, and then, He chose to answer in a totally different way. Later, when we reflect back on that situation, we know that if He had answered the way we thought, the situation would have grown worse. God knows our future; we do not. We have to trust His hand and follow the steps He has ordained for us, because as His word says, the steps of a righteous man are ordered by God.

My husband was diagnosed with a debilitating spinal cord disorder called syringomyelia in November 2009. This was one of the scariest times in my life. He went to the doctor with what we initially thought was a pulled muscle, but instead a hole (syrinx) was found in the middle of his spinal cord. The next two days were a whirlwind of doctors, neurologists, MRIs, and words we could not pronounce. Fear and worry began to, not just creep in, but totally engulf me as the what-if's, diagnosis, surgeries, and so forth were explained to us. The more I researched it, the more I became so scared of this disorder. All we knew to do was pray—pray for God to control this disorder and pray for God to control our fears. As of today, by the grace of God, my husband has still not developed any symptoms! Praise the Lord! We have not had to face ANY of the fears given upon diagnosis. While the syrinx (hole) is still there, we are still praying for a miracle from God to close the hole. However, we are so grateful that God has protected him thus far and continues to show us He is in control.

Will there be times in our life when we are in need of something? Absolutely! That is when God gives us what we need right then—faith. I often think about those who are Christians and going through trials. Where would they be if they did not have faith in God? What is more tragic in life than to be in the worst storm of your life and not have faith? The God who created all cares for us, our needs, and our wants. By faith, we say, "The Lord is my shepherd; I have all that I need."

My reflections of my personal journey

_____

_____

_____

_____

_____

_____

_____

_____

Day 12

*How precious to me are your thoughts,
God! How vast is the sum of them!
Psalms 139:17 (NIV)*

onight, my husband and I had the privilege to distribute Thanksgiving food baskets to families in our church that are struggling this year. Our church, as well as people in the community, came together to bless these families. No one, except the staff of the church, knew the families visited. These families have encountered various trials this year—surgeries, losing jobs, starting life over completely. One family had lost everything except one car, including their house. These families combined had 15 children under the age 18. Some were in awe that our church cared that much and were very thankful. While I am sure every family was very appreciative, I do think a couple were shocked, perhaps uncomfortable, they were visited.

As we shared the baskets with the families, some openly discussed their trials. However, even through their current circumstances, they still see the blessings God has bestowed upon them. With each one, I am reminded of how blessed I am. Each morning I awake in a house with my family and go to my job, I am reminded of God's goodness and blessings. I have absolutely no right to complain about anything in my life! I am an heir to the King of Kings and the Lord of Lords. Everything in my life has been provided by my Father. Sometimes, we have to step back and not ask for anything but bask in His love and goodness. As His thoughts are on us, so should ours be on Him.

My reflections of my personal journey

_____

_____

_____

_____

_____

_____

_____

_____

_____

_____

_____

Day 13

And Jesus said to him, "'If You can?' All things are possible to him who believes." Immediately the boy's father cried out and said, "I do believe; help my unbelief."
Mark 9:23-24 (NASB)

When God gives us a promise, we know that His promise is true and will come to pass. Oftentimes when we pray for a need, we initially have strong faith. As time passes and the need has not been met yet, our faith tends to weaken. Why does our faith weaken when we know His promise does not! His words and promises are true!

Through this 30-day journey, I would have 3-4 days with no spasms and get so excited. Then, the spasms would return. I had to remind myself that God directed me to write this journal, and I had several confirmations throughout. I truly had to work on keeping my faith strong. Paul states in 2 Timothy 4:7, "I have fought a good fight, I have finished my course, I have kept the faith." We need to make sure we finish our course!

Faith must be continuous. Faith must be consistent. Faith cannot be strong only in good days; it must be strong every day. Faith cannot be strong only when we are feeling well, but we must keep our faith strong during the pain. Regardless if the situation seems positive or grim, we must keep faith in our faith. Faith should not ride on emotions. No matter what you are facing today, strive to strengthen your faith, to make it stronger with each day.

My reflections of my personal journey

_____

_____

_____

_____

_____

_____

_____

_____

_____

_____

_____

_____

Day 14

But they that wait upon the LORD shall renew their strength; they shall mount up with wings as eagles; they shall run, and not be weary; and they shall walk, and not faint.

Isaiah 40:31

*T*his Bible verse is one of the most familiar verses in the Bible. It is actually my husband's favorite Bible verse. What a splendid image we can gather from this—to soar with eagles that represent strength and beauty, to soar above all the cares and struggles of this world and fly in His presence. The NIV translation of this verse states, "But those that *hope* in the Lord." What a peace of mind we have in that our hope is in the Lord!

Countless verses and songs have depicted the hope we have in our Lord. The old hymn states: *My hope is built on nothing less, Than Jesus Christ, my righteousness; I dare not trust the sweetest frame, But wholly lean on Jesus' name.* Mark Lowry and Bruce Carroll wrote a song that beautifully reflects this hope[2]:

There is hope, so hold on, there is hope
God has sent me here to tell you,
there is hope
And He knows just what you're
going through
And what the future holds
As long as Jesus lives ... there is hope

I cannot fathom going through life, with its struggles and trials, without having a relationship with God, without having His grace, mercy, and hope. At times when your faith seems diminished, you can rest in knowing your hope is in Him. *There is hope, so hold on.*

My reflections of my personal journey

_____

_____

_____

_____

_____

_____

_____

_____

_____

Day 15

"For I know the plans I have for you,"
declares the LORD, "plans to prosper
you and not to harm you, plans to give
you hope and a future."
Jeremiah 29:11 (NIV)

Forty percent of what people worry about never comes to fruition. Thirty percent of worries have already come to pass and cannot be changed. Twelve percent is worry about our health, and ten percent is miscellaneous worry of petty things. Therefore, only eight percent of worries should actually be considered as true worry.[1] Why then, do we always worry? When we get a call from the doctor's office about a result of a test, when our bills exceed our pay check that week, when we do not know what else to do to handle a certain situation, we tend to worry and worry and worry.

There are many strategies to help you cope with worries and anxieties. However, the number one strategy is to turn to God. He has clearly said, *declared,* that He has a plan for us, plans to prosper us, plans to give us hope and a future. Psalms 139:16 (NIV) states, "...all the days ordained for me were written in your book before one of them came to be." In our mother's womb, He knew us and chose a plan for us. God sometimes reveals His plan as a map for us; sometimes, only a few steps are revealed at one time. If we follow His plan as He unveils it to us, we have no reason to fear or worry. He is in complete control! Seek Him today to follow the plan He has for you. Give your worries to the One who can subside all fear.

My reflections of my personal journey

_____

_____

_____

_____

_____

_____

_____

_____

_____

_____

_____

_____

Personal Journal

*E*ach night as I read Scripture and wrote the devotionals, I recorded notes about my physical being and if I had experienced any spasms that day. The following is the recording of those entries. I have placed this purposely in the middle of the devotions. As you will find after Day 15 listed below, I questioned EVERYTHING about this journey. However, I did not give up. Please do not give up on yours either!

Day 1—I started this journal tonight. I had a spasm earlier this morning at 6 a.m.

However, I am praying for a complete night of sleep.

Day 2—I woke up this morning singing a song, "Lord, You have been faithful to me." However, this was a difficult day. One of my closest friends died this morning after battling cancer for four years. On a rare Sunday morning when I was in the adult service, Pastor spoke about going through a faith crisis, Habakkuk 1. This sermon was one that I needed to hear and confirmed this journey I have begun. No spasm during the night or all day—41 hours and counting!!!

Day 3—I had to take a nitroglycerin this morning, but the spasm was not very severe! Praise God!

Day 4—I had to take a nitroglycerin during the night, and the pain was bad enough that I had to wake my husband. God bless him for what he has had to go through! Today was hard as I said goodbye to one of my close friends. Even unto her death, her faith never waivered! Oh, to be more like her.

Day 5—I had a mild spasm today but did not have to take nitroglycerin as I was able to endure. My spasms are not life threatening, just very painful. If they were life threatening, I would not omit the medicine that the doctor prescribed through God-given wisdom.

Day 6—No spasms today! Praise the Lord!!!

Day 7—Another day and still no spasms, even though I did not eat lunch until 1:30 p.m. What a blessing!

Day 8—Three straight days with no spasms!

Day 9—I had one spasm during the night which required medication. Still claiming I am healed!

Day 10—I had another spasm in the middle of the night.

Day 11—I had a spasm during the day.

Day 12—No spasms!!!

Day 13—Thanksgiving Day. Thankful for no spasms!

Day 14—I had one spasm, but waited it out without taking nitroglycerin.

Day 15—I had another spasm during the night. Hoping, *believing*, this is my last one!

At one time during this journey, I began to question if I understood what God had spoken to my heart. The spasms had come back more frequently than on the onset of this journey. I confided in my dad about my weakening faith. He reminded me that I was on an uphill climb on this mountain. The next day, I had a spasm and began crying out to God in prayer. As I was praying,

"*Everything I Need*" by Kutless came on the radio[3]:

When every step is so hard to take
And all of my hope is fading away
When life is a mountain that I cannot climb
You carry me, Jesus carry me.
You Are strength in my weakness
You are the refuge I seek
You are everything in my time of need
You are everything, You are
everything I need.

Beginning Day 16—I have stopped documenting the spasms. I have only taken a few nitroglycerin over the past days. I am going to stop counting what spasms I have had and be thankful for what I have not had!

As you have been going through this journey, you may have encountered moments where your faith was weakened. Take this pause and remind yourself that the promises that God spoke to you through the first 15 days are still true. Take a moment to refresh, and then continue on to Day 16.

Day 16

*Have I not commanded you? Be strong
and courageous. Do not be terrified;
do not be discouraged, for the LORD
your God will be with you wherever
you go."*

Joshua 1:9 (NIV)

Finally, you realize what God's direction is for you at this time of your life.
Everything seems to be going great! You're
getting stronger, you're seeing things more
clearly, and everything is starting to look so
much brighter. You are about to reach the

top of your mountain! Then, you notice that your situation is not changing as quickly as it first seemed. You realize you are no closer to the top of the mountain today than you were yesterday. Then, you realize you may have backed up a few steps. Your situation is not getting better. Your body is not healed yet. Your bills are still not being met. Your faith is weakening again. What is going on? Did you really know this was God's path for you? Did you understand it correctly? Did God even answer the prayer?

When God speaks to you and you know it is God, then you cling to that promise! You keep pressing forward, reaching toward the top of the mountain. You keep walking your faith walk, even if you must walk one step at a time. Keep looking for the day when you can stand over the valley you just walked through on top of the mountain—with your answer to your prayer!

My reflections of my personal journey

Day 17

Let the words of my mouth and the meditation of my heart be acceptable in Your sight, O LORD, my rock and my Redeemer.
Psalms 19:14 (NASB)

In this technology age with social media readily available and widely used, more people "read" more of what we say. We have always guarded our tongue and actions lest we hinder our Christian testimony. However, I am often blown away by the posts on social media and written word of others I read. Apparently, some people feel they can be more vocal and hide behind emails, texts, and social media posts and hold themselves less responsible for what they write than what they would actually speak to someone. I have actually posted on a social media site the following statement several times: "Let the words of my mouth and the meditations of my heart and my posts on Facebook be acceptable to you O Lord." How do we present the joy of the Lord if we consistently write negative words and negative testimonies?

In Psalms 19:14, David reminds us to guard our mouth and our heart and let it be acceptable to God. When God has promised us healing, why do we speak that we are not healed nor can we be healed? Why do we not proclaim and meditate on the promise we have received from Him? Proverbs 19:21 states that death and life are in the power of the tongue. My mother-in-law repeatedly advises to speak healing and not sickness. What are we speaking? In fact, what are we even thinking? Make sure your thoughts in your mind and hearts, your spoken and written words, clearly align with God's promise for your life. Go ahead and say it now...speak your healing! I AM HEALED!

My reflections of my personal journey

_____

_____

_____

_____

_____

_____

_____

Day 18

Immediately Jesus reached out his hand and caught him. "You of little faith," He said, "why did you doubt?"
Matthew 14:31 (NIV)

Jesus walking on water is one of the Bible lessons most of us have heard over and over. While Jesus walking on water is amazing in itself, that is not the only lesson to explore in this story. This illustration is about faith. Peter became so courageous that he began to walk on the water towards the Lord. He was actually walking on water! Peter had enough faith to step out on the water. As long as Peter kept his eyes on Jesus, his feet stayed on top of the water. However, the moment he turned his eyes away from the Master, Peter's feet began to sink. At that time, so did his faith.

The old hymn says:

> *Turn your eyes upon Jesus,*
> *Look full in His wonderful face,*
> *And the things of earth will grow*
> *strangely dim,*
> *In the light of His glory and grace.*[4]

When we turn our eyes to Him, everything else grows dim. How often do we take our eyes off of the Master and onto our situation? Each time we do this, our faith is weakened and we begin to sink. If we are driving a car and take our eyes off the road for even a short period of time, we will steer off the road and possibly crash. When we take our eyes off Jesus, our spiritual soul will also crash. We must keep our eyes, and thus our faith, on Jesus. I never want Him to ask me, "Why did you doubt?"

My reflections of my personal journey

_____

_____

_____

_____

_____

_____

_____

_____

_____

_____

_____

Day 19

Peter fairly exploded with his good news: "It's God's own truth, nothing could be plainer: God plays no favorites! It makes no difference who you are or where you're from—if you want God and are ready to do as he says, the door is open. The Message he sent to the children of Israel—that through Jesus Christ everything is being put together again—well, he's doing it everywhere, among everyone.

Acts 10:34-38 (The Message)

easure up...compare...rate...rank. We often live our lives by looking in the windows of others. Why do we compare and judge elements of our lives by what we perceive others to have or be? Throughout my career as a college instructor, I have encountered countless students that have severe low self-esteem, and I even see this same confidence issue in young teens today. One motto I have always lived by is, "There is no one in the world better than me." Before you judge and say that is prideful, let me explain. This does not mean that I am better than anyone else. It simply means that I am a child of God, created just as He designed, and living the life He breathed in me.

Acts 10:34 reminds us that God is no respecter of persons. We are all His children, and He loves us all the same. He longs for that relationship with each of us. He cares about every need in our lives, no matter how small, and no matter what the need. Oftentimes, I thought that my spasms did not compare to the sickness, strife, heartache, and death we witness daily. However, I am reminded that God is Jehovhah-Shammah, the omnipresent being—the One who is in control of *ALL* of our lives simultaneously, without error.

Make your petition known to God today. After all, He knows your need before you even request. He will answer you—in His time, His will, and His way—every time!

My reflections of my personal journey

_____

_____

_____

_____

_____

_____

_____

_____

_____

_____

_____

_____

_____

_____

_____

_____

_____

_____

_____

_____

Day 20

*Don't worry about anything; instead,
pray about everything. Tell God what
you need, and thank him for all he
has done.*
Philippians 4:6 (NLT)

The phone call. The visit to the doctor's office. The meeting with your
boss. The knock at the door. Any of these
one things can completely change your
life. Any of these can cause your mind to
race, your heart to pound, and your breath
to become shallow. Sometimes, we do not

know what to say or do. God's word tells us over and over to cast our cares upon the Lord, to make our petitions known to him, and not to worry or be anxious. However, our human nature sometimes supersedes our spiritual soul.

When fear, worry, and anxiety come upon us, we need to refocus our thoughts and sight, not on our circumstances, but on the One who is in complete control! We need to release our burden, fear, and worry to God and rejoice in knowing He will carry it for us. A new phrase in our society today that people say is, "I got this." This is not a new phrase for God. He has ALWAYS had this!

Do not miss one important word in Philippians 4:6—thanksgiving! With thanksgiving, present your request to God. Thank Him for who He is and what He has done. Thank Him for what He is going to do.

Thank Him for being in complete control of the situations in your life.

What circumstance do you need to turn over to God? Give it to Him. Let Him be in control, and then, thank Him!

My reflections of my personal journey

_____

_____

_____

_____

_____

_____

_____

_____

_____

_____

_____

_____

Day 21

"Come to me, all you who are weary and burdened, and I will give you rest."

Matthew 11:28 (NIV)

How often the busyness of our lives keeps us from the rest we need. With work, children's activities, family, friends, and yes, even church activities, we often find ourselves filling in too many hours of the day and neglecting ourselves. We must find time to rest our bodies. Countless studies have proven over and over how lack of sleep and stress can affect the body. If we are not physically fit, how can we be spiritually fit? Physical ailments will alter our spiritual minds. We need to not only physically rest; we need to spiritually rest.

God commands us to come unto Him, and He will give us rest. This rest is more than just slumber sleep. This rest is a peace that overwhelms us. It lifts our heavy burdens. It restores our joy. It gives us clarity and understanding. Oh, run to Him, lie at His feet, breathe His presence, feel His heart beat, and rest.

My reflections of my personal journey

_____

_____

_____

_____

_____

_____

Day 22

Finally, brothers, whatever is true, whatever is noble, whatever is right, whatever is pure, whatever is lovely, whatever is admirable—if anything is excellent or praiseworthy—think about such things.

Philippians 4:8 (NIV)

The Bible tells us there is power in the tongue. Therefore, we watch closely what we say. Do you know that the mind is even as powerful? Our thoughts can be our most dominating enemy. Our thoughts are in constant battle with our faith. We must remember that our thoughts are of a human nature. These thoughts are full of worry, regret, fear, uncertainty, self-doubt, and so forth. Certainly these thoughts are not thoughts that are true, pure, or holy. Philippians 4:8 reminds us to think on holy things.

When we are going through physical, emotional, or spiritual sickness, we must engulf our minds with thoughts of God our Healer. We must remember that sickness is not our god; strife is not our god. These thoughts have no place in our minds. Our God is a God who is alive, who reigns! He is the only one true living God. When we worship and praise Him, our hearts and minds are full of thoughts about Him, not our sickness. We must dwell on thoughts of His Majesty—our Healer, our Protector, our Provider! He is a God of excellence. He is worthy to be praised!

My reflections of my personal journey

_____

_____

_____

_____

_____

_____

_____

_____

_____

_____

_____

_____

_____

_____

Day 23

My help comes from the LORD, Who made heaven and earth. He will not allow your foot to slip; He who keeps you will not slumber.
Psalm 121:2-3 (NASB)

Sometimes as children, we would fear about sounds in the middle of the night. We worried that our parents did not hear them because they were asleep. Would they wake up to protect us if something bad was happening? Do you remember any of those nights as a child? If you are a parent now, do your children have those same fears? How do you reassure them that you are there to protect them from harm? Our Father God should not have to prove to us He is our Protector. We should not have to be convinced! He has proven Himself faithful time and time again. He does not slumber nor does He divert his attention away from us—never!

Even though we know God is always there to protect and shelter us, we sometimes find ourselves struggling. Sometimes, we wonder where God is. Is He moving in this situation? Is He healing our body? Is He listening? When Jesus was on the cross, He cried, "My God, My God, why hast thou forsaken me." God the Son even questioned if God the Father had forsaken Him, even though He knew God had not. We must not beat ourselves down if our faith is weakened momentarily. What is more important is that we begin to rebuild our faith if this happens. Our help comes from the Lord. Our faith is built in trusting the One who does not allow us to slip, fall, or be moved. Our faith is in the One who never sleeps nor slumbers.

My reflections of my personal journey

_____

_____

_____

_____

_____

_____

_____

_____

_____

_____

_____

_____

Day 24

In the day of my trouble I shall call upon You, For You will answer me.
Psalm 86:7 (NASB)

*L*istening and hearing are often used interchangeably. However, these two words are not the same. As a wife, I know my husband does not always "hear" what I say. Of course, he calls it "selective hearing." It isn't that he does not hear me; he just may not be listening. Sometimes, we hear people talking to us, but we do not listen. We do not reflect on what they are saying or on what they are not saying. We do not act upon what we hear.

Our Father always listens to us. He listens to our audible words, the thoughts in our minds, and the cries of our hearts. He does not merely hear us; He listens! No word that we utter will rest on a deaf ear with Him. He knows what we are going to say or pray before we even say it. When we talk to Him about our needs, pray to Him about our problems, ask Him about our needed healings, He is faithful to hear us and act upon our requests.

The next time you pray or talk to God, know that He hears you. Have faith that your words are reaching the throne of Heaven, reaching the One who has all power! And...He is listening!

My reflections of my personal journey

_____

_____

_____

_____

_____

_____

_____

_____

_____

_____

_____

_____

_____

_____

_____

_____

_____

_____

_____

Day 25

I can do all things through Christ which strengtheneth me.
Philippians 4:13

think I can. I think I can. I think I can. We are all familiar with the story of the little engine that could. A little engine that took on a task, an impossible task, that other larger engines had feared. The engine completed this great task while repeating the words, "I think I can." Then, as the task was accomplished, the engine began chanting, "I thought I could.

I thought I could." Many people use this story to encourage others.

As Christians, we find rest in knowing that we do not have to "think" we can. We *know* that with Christ, who gives us strength, we *can* do all things! If we are in God's will, carrying forth His plan for our life, we can do any task He sets before us. We can have the confidence that we can do it to completion.

In our children's department, we often have practice with the children for dramas or musicals. During these practices, I strive to ensure two things. One is that no child says, "I cannot do this." The other is that all of the children know that it is all for His glory, not theirs or the teachers.

If God can empower us to do things, simple tasks in our small worlds, how much more is He able to do Himself? When we gain perspective of how powerful God is and how big our God is, we can then fully trust Him to supply our needs. We can have faith that He can heal us and our situations—whether physically, emotionally, or spiritually. He will do all things which strengthens us!

My reflections of my personal journey

_____

_____

_____

_____

_____

_____

_____

_____

_____

_____

Day 26

For we are his workmanship, cre-
ated in Christ Jesus unto good works,
which God hath before ordained that
we should walk in them.
Ephesians 2:10

Sometimes we feel that we are in a maze. We think we have found an opening in our journey, and it is merely another dead end. In many areas of our lives, we do not know which way to go anymore. At times, we get this feeling when facing trials in our life—whether it is a family member, financial problems, or a physical ailment. We seek professionals—doctors, bankers, lawyers, and such—to help us in our time of need. While all wisdom comes from above and we need to seek these professionals, we can never lose our faith and trust in our Father. Our Father owns the cattle on a thousand hills; He can meet our financial needs. He is the author and finisher of our faith; He can guide and direct and protect our loved ones. Our doctor may not know how to fix our body, but the One that made it does.

God desires for us to live under His blessings. We all have a purpose that God wants us to carry out! Sometimes, we must endure trials, but His grace is sufficient for us! We must remember that we are God's workmanship. We are created to do good works, and God continuously prepares us for this. Have faith in Him, trust Him, and rest in knowing that God is preparing us in advance for what He needs us to do.

My reflections of my personal journey

_____

_____

_____

_____

_____

_____

_____

_____

_____

_____

_____

_____

_____

_____

_____

Day 27

It's impossible to please God apart from faith. And why? Because anyone who wants to approach God must believe both that he exists and that he cares enough to respond to those who seek him.

Hebrews 11:6 (The Message)

God created man to worship Him. To stay in God's will for our lives, we must worship Him, love Him, develop a relationship with Him, and keep His commandments. We have been well versed on each of these; we abide by these. Sometimes, we neglect other directives we find from the Bible—to love our neighbors, to share the Gospel, and to have faith. Yes, the Bible commands us to have faith—it is not an option. Hebrews 11:6 states that if we do not have faith, we are not pleasing God. If we claim we know Him and believe that He exists, He will reward us.

We often remind ourselves to do what is right—do not lie, do not steal, not to put anything above our God. To not do right is to sin. We must constantly remind ourselves that having faith is doing what is right—it is a must. At times our faith may weaken, but we have to continuously build it—keeping our mind on what is pure and Holy—the promise of God.

During the two-year period of having internal spasms, I lost my faith that God could and would heal me. I had to repent of my sin, the unbelief I had in my Father healing my body. Through the process of writing this journal, I have once again found peace in the Healer. My prayer is that you, too, can find such peace.

My reflections of my personal journey

_____

_____

_____

_____

_____

_____

_____

_____

_____

_____

_____

Day 28

Now unto him that is able to do exceeding abundantly above all that we ask or think, according to the power that worketh in us.
Ephesians 3:20

*H*ow awesome is our God! How endless is His love for us! He is all-knowing, all-powerful, and He is also our Abba Father! Oh, how He loves us!

Since my daughter was born, she has captured and held my husband's heart. She has a way, that only a daughter can, of asking him to do whatever, where he cannot say "no." He goes through great lengths to ensure she is happy. Oh, the love a father has for a daughter is immeasurable. How much greater love does our Abba Father have for us? He loves us so much that He died on the cross for us!

God should not be limited! We often expect too less of God than He has planned to give. So often, we give up too early on His promise. Doubt enters in where faith should dwell. We are children of the King, heirs to the throne. We should expect what is ours and that He is willing to give it to us. He is able to do well beyond what we can imagine or ask. Exceedingly, abundantly, above all we could ask. Right now, ask God for what you need and expect wonders!

My reflections of my personal journey

Day 29

God blesses those who patiently endure testing and temptation. Afterward they will receive the crown of life that God has promised to those who love him.
James 1:12 (NLT)

The Bible presents God as the Potter and us as the clay. Many times over, God will mold us and make us into what He desires for us to be—to fulfill His purpose for our lives. The fire can often get very hot during this refining process. The heat may seem like more than we can bear. However, we must always realize that we are in the hands of the Potter. We cannot see the finished product, but God sees it. It is beautiful and perfect.

Think back over your life, when you have gone through trials, when your faith seemed small, when you felt there was no answer. But then, your prayers were answered, your life restored, and you were even at a higher place than before your trial began. Only after reflecting back on these times, do we see God's purpose. Only then, do we understand the reasoning and what God used this trial to accomplish.

As you go through a trial, know that the Potter is molding you with every move. His hands never leave you but are carefully forming you into His craftsmanship. Through the molding, bending, and even emerging in the fire, God is using this trial to make you stronger. Know that you can prevail during this time. When you do, your reward will be great!

My reflections of my personal journey

_____
_____
_____
_____
_____
_____
_____
_____
_____
_____
_____
_____
_____

Day 30

May the God of hope fill you with all joy and peace as you trust in him, so that you may overflow with hope by the power of the Holy Spirit.
Romans 15:13 (NIV)

What a comfort in knowing we have faith in our today and our tomorrow. What peace there is when we trust our God with our life and situations, when we are filled with hope and faith. His Word says it, so we can claim it!

As I write Day 30 today, I had to take a nitroglycerin. It is the last one in the bottle. Even though I have available prescriptions, I believe my spasms are gone and that I do not need to refill the prescription. I have faith in my God that I am healed! Thank you, Jesus!

Through this 30-day journey of faith, my prayer is that your faith has been rebuilt. Now is the time to reflect on the past 29 days and see what God has done already in your life. While you may or may not have seen your prayer answered yet, know that it is on its way in His time. Through studying His word, speaking with Him, fellowshipping with Him, believing in Him, and loving Him, I trust you have drawn closer to God through this journey.

Keep going forward, keep trusting, keep believing, and keep building your faith!

My reflections of my personal journey

_____

_____

_____

_____

_____

_____

_____

_____

_____

_____

_____

_____

_____

_____

_____

_____

_____

_____

_____

_____

Endnotes

[1] Nightingale, Earl. *The EssencTe of Success*. Lightning Source Inc, 2007.

[2] Lowry, Mark and Carroll, Bruce. "There is Hope." *This Is the Life*. Word Records, 1994.

[3] Sumrall, Jon Micah and Lubben, Dave. "Everything I Need." *It is Well: A Worship Album*. Bec Recordings, 2009.

[4] Lemmel, Helen H. "Turn Your Eyes Upon Jesus." Public Domain, 1922.